THE BLACKNESS OF DARKNESS

...What The World Wasn't Meant To See, But Must Know!

Emma Abbey

The Blackness of Darkness

...What The World Wasn't Meant To See, But Must Know!

Emma Abbey

Copyright

THE BLACKNESS OF DARKNESS

…What The World Wasn't Meant To See, But Must Know!

First Edition

Copyright © 2025 by Emma Abbey

All rights reserved under the international and Pan-American copyright conventions. No part of this book may be reproduced or transmitted in any form or by any means, electronic or mechanical, including photocopying, or by any information, storage and retrieval system, without permission in writing from the copyright owner.

ISBN: 978-1-257-97641-6

Table of Contents

Copyright 3

Foreword 8

Dedication 10

INTRODUCTION 11

   When Shadows Speak Louder Than Light 11

Author's Note 14

   CHAPTER ONE 16

      The Seduction of Silence 16

      The Unholy Comfort 17

      Inherited Quiet 18

      The Business of Darkness 19

      When You Speak, You Break Spells 19

      The Cost of Truth, The Price of Peace 20

      A Final Reflection 21

   CHAPTER TWO 22

      Architects of the Abyss 22

      More Than a Moment 23

      The Invisible Builders 24

      System Over Sin 25

    The Face of the System 26

    Why It Still Stands 27

    How to Tear It Down 27

    Closing Reflection 28

CHAPTER THREE 29

    Darkness Has a Language 29

    The Language of Silence 30

    The Code of Control 31

    When Culture Becomes a Cage 32

    The Symbols We Ignore 33

    The Performance of Peace 34

    Learning a New Language 35

    Final Reflection 36

CHAPTER FOUR 36

    Living in the Shadows 36

    The Shadow Life 37

    The Architecture of Internal Darkness 38

    Functional Shadows 39

    What the Shadows Feed On 40

    The Cost of Staying Hidden 41

    How to Come Out 42

Final Reflection 44

CHAPTER FIVE 45

The Whisper of Light 45

Not All Light Is Loud 46

When Light Finds You 47

The Light Doesn't Lie 48

Stories of Escape 49

The Fear of Stepping Out 50

The Choice to Follow 51

Final Reflection 52

CHAPTER SEVEN 54

Becoming a Light-Bearer 54

What Light-Bearers Look Like 55

The Cost of Carrying Light 56

How to Carry the Light 57

Be Light in the Way You Were Designed 58

CHAPTER EIGHT 60

Light Was Made for War 60

Warriors Don't Always Wear Armor 61

What Light Destroys 62

Why Light Must Be Fierce 63

You Are Now the Light 64

Final Charge 65

Foreword

There are books that entertain.
There are books that inform.
And then - every once in a while - a book comes along that *awakens*.

The Blackness of Darkness is such a book.

In a world addicted to image and allergic to truth, Emma Abbey has dared to do what few are willing: speak plainly about the systems, secrets, and silent agreements that keep individuals, families, and even spiritual communities trapped in bondage.

This is not a self-help manual.
It is not a theological dissertation.
It is a spotlight — one that exposes what hides in plain sight and names what many are too afraid to acknowledge.

With poetic honesty, prophetic insight, and piercing clarity, Abbey guides us through the shadows — not to scare us, but to *set us free*. He shows that darkness is not just the absence of light, but often the presence of structure: structured silence, structured abuse, structured oppression.

What makes this work powerful is not only its content, but its cost.

This book was not written from comfort — it was written from confrontation.

It is the result of wrestling, of seeing too much to stay silent, and of deciding that comfort is not more valuable than truth.

As you read these pages, prepare to be disrupted.
Prepare to rethink what you thought was "normal."
Prepare to revisit wounds you buried — not to relive them, but to finally heal them.

More than anything, prepare to be *activated*.

Because the darkness does not die in silence.
It dies when someone turns on the light.

And Abbey has done exactly that.

May this book be a torch in your hand —
And may you never again pretend not to see.

- Emma Abbey
Author, Advocate, Truth-Teller

Dedication

To the ones who suffered in silence.

Who carried light in their hearts while walking through unspeakable darkness.

Who were never believed, but never broke.

This is for you.

You were seen. You still are.

INTRODUCTION

When Shadows Speak Louder Than Light

Darkness is not merely the absence of light.
It is not just a color, a void, or a time of day.
Darkness is a presence. It is a force.
And in today's world, it is organized, intentional, and disturbingly effective.

We often speak of the "light" as the symbol of all that is good — truth, purity, healing, clarity. But what if we've underestimated the intelligence and design of darkness? What if, behind the curtains of society, religion, politics, media, and even family life, something ancient and malevolent is orchestrating shadows — not with chaos, but with precision?

The Blackness of Darkness is not about superstition or fear-mongering. It is a revelation.
It is a flashlight in the cellar of human experience — spiritual, psychological, and systemic.

This book is for the man who senses that his addiction isn't just chemical — it's spiritual.

It's for the woman who smiles in public but bleeds in private.
It's for the adult who grew up under the rule of secrecy, silence, and shame.
And it's for the seeker — the one who knows that truth exists beyond what the eyes can see.

Darkness speaks, but not in words.
It speaks through control, suppression, manipulation, and confusion. It wraps itself in culture. It hides in religion. It thrives in systems that reward silence and punish exposure.

Here's the hard truth:
The world is not only broken because of bad people doing evil things.
It is broken because good people pretend not to see them.

Behind the laughter on television, behind the sanitized sermons, behind the well-dressed institutions and perfectly curated images, something festers. Something whispers. Something plots. This book pulls back that curtain.

You will not finish this journey the same.
You may feel disturbed. That's okay.
You may feel awakened. That's the point.

Because *when shadows speak louder than light*, it is not light that has failed — it is the silence of those who carry it.

"Darkness only wins where silence is sacred. This book is the noise it fears."

Author's Note

This book was not written out of curiosity - it was born out of conviction.

For years, I watched as people danced around the truth, afraid to name what they sensed. I saw institutions protect appearances while their foundations rotted in secrecy. I met strong men, broken by invisible chains. I listened to brave women speak in hushed tones about pain too heavy for the daylight. And within me grew a holy unrest - a fire that refused to be silent any longer.

The Blackness of Darkness is not fiction. It is the mirror we often avoid.
It is my attempt to put language to the unspeakable.

To unmask the smiling devils.

To shine light on the inner systems - spiritual, emotional, institutional - that thrive in darkness.

This is not a comfortable read.
It's not meant to be.

But if you are weary of shallow answers… if you have questioned what lies beneath the surface… if you've ever asked, *"Why does evil seem so organized?"* - This book is for you.

I write not as one above the darkness, but as one who has wrestled within it — who has learned that to shine a light is to become a threat. And still, I write.

Because the truth is:

Light was never meant to decorate the room. It was meant to confront it.

If this book awakens you, disturbs you, or stirs something you can't explain — then it has done its job. May you not only see the blackness of darkness, but rise above it with the courage to expose, reveal, and live free.

With light and truth,

Emma Abbey

CHAPTER ONE

The Seduction of Silence

There's a reason darkness prefers silence. Not just because silence is quiet—but because silence is safe.

You see, evil doesn't always knock down doors. It often whispers. It negotiates. It doesn't demand your soul all at once—it asks you to just *keep quiet. Don't talk. Don't ask too many questions. Don't make it worse.* And slowly, without knowing it, you become a gatekeeper of your own prison.

Silence is seductive.

It appears noble at first—like peacekeeping, like maturity, like strength. You tell yourself, "This isn't the time," or "It's not my business," or "Let me just pray about it." And while those words may sound spiritual, they can become spiritual camouflage for cowardice.

Somewhere along the way, we mistook stillness for strength and silence for wisdom.

But in truth, silence has built more tombs than truth ever has.

The Unholy Comfort

There's a strange kind of comfort in not speaking up.
When you don't name the thing that haunts you, you can pretend it's not there.
When you don't call out the predator in the room, you don't risk becoming a target.
When you keep your questions to yourself, you don't lose favor.

This is the unholy comfort of silence.
It protects your image, but it imprisons your soul.

Entire communities, families, and churches have been built on this lie: "We don't talk about such things here."
So we dress our wounds in religion. We hide abuse behind titles. We bury betrayal beneath cultural tradition.
And darkness watches... smiling.

Because the longer you say nothing, the louder it grows.

Inherited Quiet

Silence is not just something we practice — it's something we inherit.

Many of us were raised under the rule of silence.
As children, we were taught not to ask certain questions.
Not to challenge authority.
Not to cry too loudly.
Not to speak unless spoken to.

And when trauma came, silence was our inheritance.
"Don't bring shame to this family."
"Don't speak against God's servant."
"Don't air your dirty laundry."

But what if the silence *is* the dirt?

What if the very thing we were told not to say is the thing that needs to be said most?

We were conditioned to believe that silence preserves peace.
But in truth, silence often preserves pain.

The Business of Darkness

Make no mistake: silence is a business.

It is bought with bribes, reinforced by fear, maintained by guilt, and sold as wisdom. It's why companies cover up scandals. Why governments suppress whistleblowers. Why spiritual leaders silence dissenters. Why families ostracize truth-tellers.

Darkness is not disorganized—it is strategic.

And its favorite tool isn't violence or chaos.

It is silence.

Silence keeps the predator on the pulpit.
Silence keeps the abused in the pew.
Silence keeps corruption in the boardroom.
Silence keeps the victim at the dinner table—smiling.

Until someone decides to speak.

When You Speak, You Break Spells

The moment you break your silence, the spell shatters.

You don't even have to be eloquent. You don't have to have all the evidence.

Just saying the words — *"That happened to me,"* or *"This is not okay,"* — begins to tear down the walls that darkness depends on.

Speaking isn't just expression.
It's exorcism.

There's power in testimony. Not just because it heals you—but because it exposes what's been hiding in others.
One voice creates an echo. An echo becomes a movement. And that movement becomes a light.

This chapter isn't a call to be loud for loudness' sake. It's a call to be honest.
Because what you refuse to say, you silently serve.

The Cost of Truth, The Price of Peace

Let's be real. Speaking truth costs something.

You may lose your place in the circle. You may be called dramatic, rebellious, disloyal.
You may be misunderstood. Misquoted. Rejected.

But the price of peace built on silence is much greater.

That peace will rot from the inside.
It will devour your joy.
It will eat your dreams.
It will chain your voice.

You are not betraying anyone by telling the truth.
You are betraying yourself by not telling it.

A Final Reflection

So let me ask you:

What have you *not* said?
What truth sits heavy on your tongue but never makes it out?
What pain have you normalized just to keep others comfortable?

If silence has seduced you, it's time to break the spell.

Because the longer you stay quiet, the darker it gets.

And the darker it gets, the harder it is to find your way back.

When you light a candle in a silent room, everything starts to speak.
May this chapter be that candle.

CHAPTER TWO

Architects of the Abyss

Darkness does not simply exist.
It is *designed*.

And behind its veil stand the architects.

These are not the monsters of bedtime stories. Not always the ones you expect, cloaked in shadows or dripping with obvious malice. No, the true architects of darkness are often refined. Polished. Smiling. Sitting at conference tables. Preaching from pulpits. Writing laws. Leading prayer meetings. Signing deals.

They do not always destroy with swords.
They build systems.

And then they disappear into them.

More Than a Moment

When we think of evil, we often think of acts — the murder, the betrayal, the theft, the lie. But darkness at its most potent is rarely a single moment. It is a machinery.

Someone builds it.
Someone funds it.
Someone protects it.
Someone calls it "normal."

Evil thrives not because bad things happen — but because bad systems are built to make them happen *repeatedly*… and make us forget they're bad.

That's the difference between an accident and architecture.
Accidents happen once.
Architecture sustains.

The Invisible Builders

The architects of the abyss know how to hide in plain sight.

They speak in codes:
"This is just how we do things here."
"It's always been this way."
"Don't question authority."

They create cultures where exposure is sin, and compliance is holiness.

You'll find them in family lines, where abuse is inherited and no one speaks.
In religious institutions, where charisma is weaponized and repentance is optional for the powerful.
In politics, where promises are made with straight faces and broken behind gold-plated doors.
In the corporate world, where people are just numbers on spreadsheets — bodies traded for profit.

These are the men and women who draft the blueprints of decay, not always with evil intent, but with cold detachment from consequences.
And what's worse — many of them *believe they are doing good.*

That's what makes them dangerous.

System Over Sin

The individual sin is not what shakes societies.
It's when sin becomes a structure.

It's when oppression is written into policy.
When exploitation is legitimized by paperwork.
When silence is rewarded and questioning is punished.
When the wound becomes a business model — and healing becomes unprofitable.

Look deeper.

Look beyond the scandal to the scaffolding.
Who benefits when nothing changes?
Who profits from keeping people bound?
Who designed the house that keeps collapsing — and why do we keep rebuilding it with the same blueprint?

The abyss was not born.
It was *engineered*.

The Face of the System

Sometimes, the architect is not a person — it's a mindset.

A generational belief. A tradition gone sour. A doctrine twisted just enough to cage the soul but still sound holy.

For example:

- In a society where women are blamed for the violence against them, the abyss was designed.
- In a workplace where silence is the only way to survive, someone built that silence.
- In homes where love is earned through obedience but never given freely, the blueprint was laid long before the children arrived.

The face of the system is not always cruel. It can be kind. Gentle. Fatherly. Respectable.

Which is why so many never notice the darkness until they're drowning in it.

Why It Still Stands

The architects are brilliant, not just because they build —
but because they delegate the maintenance.

They make you believe the system is *yours*.
That your silence is wisdom.
That your suffering is loyalty.
That your obedience is righteousness.

So the oppressed become the defenders of their own chains.

Whole generations guard doors they were never meant to stand behind.
They punish anyone who knocks.
They turn away the light.

Because the system has convinced them:
"This darkness is all you'll ever know."
"This abyss is home."

How to Tear It Down

You don't destroy the abyss by attacking the walls.
You go for the blueprint.

You question the rules everyone obeys but no one remembers who wrote.
You challenge the language that keeps people bound.
You listen to the voices that were silenced.
You give names to the unseen things.

Sometimes it starts with one question:
"Who taught us this?"

Then another:
"Why are we still doing it?"

And finally:
"What would it cost to break free?"

When enough people ask those questions, the system shakes.
When enough light hits the structure, the architects scatter.

Not all battles need swords.
Some just need clarity.

Closing Reflection

You're not crazy.
You're not weak.
You're not rebellious for questioning the system.

You're waking up.

You're seeing the blueprint for what it is — not sacred, not untouchable, not permanent.

And once you see the architect, you stop bowing to the building.

Some darkness isn't accidental.
It was drawn, drafted, and delivered on purpose.
And it's time to start unbuilding it.

CHAPTER THREE

Darkness Has a Language

Darkness doesn't always scream.
It doesn't always arrive with drums or gunpowder or raised voices.
More often than not, it slips in unnoticed — not because it's silent, but because it speaks in a language we've learned to ignore.

Yes, darkness speaks.
And it speaks *fluently*.

Its tongue is not just heard — it's *felt*.
Its grammar is shame.
Its vocabulary is fear.
Its punctuation is silence.

And whether we know it or not, many of us have become fluent in its dialect — not because we studied it, but because we survived by it.

The Language of Silence

The first language of darkness is silence.
Not the peaceful, restful kind. No — this is the loaded silence. The silence that holds secrets like corpses in locked closets.

It says things like:

- "We don't talk about that here."
- "You know how they get."
- "Let it go — it's in the past."

But beneath those words, another message speaks:

- "If you open your mouth, we'll turn on you."
- "Truth makes people uncomfortable. And you owe them comfort."
- "No one will believe you anyway."

This silence isn't empty — it's heavy. It communicates exactly what darkness wants: *Obey. Hide. Disappear.*

The Code of Control

Darkness also has its own alphabet of control.

It uses *guilt* as a leash.
It dresses *manipulation* as loyalty.
It names *fear* as "respect."

It teaches people how to speak around the truth without ever confronting it. How to look away without feeling guilty. How to conform while pretending to be free.

You'll hear it in family meetings where everyone talks, but nothing is *said*.
You'll hear it in sermons that shout about grace but never

confront abuse.

You'll hear it in boardrooms where problems are "flagged," but no one dares name who caused them.

Darkness has mastered euphemism.
It will never say "slavery." It will say "order."
It will never say "oppression." It will say "structure."
It will never say "fear." It will say "obedience."

When Culture Becomes a Cage

Every culture has unspoken rules - customs passed down not through law, but through tone, expression, and what is rewarded or punished.

And some of those customs were born in the dark.

You know you're in a culture of darkness when:

- Pain is normalized.
- Doubt is punished.
- Conformity is praised more than honesty.
- People know the truth — but pretend not to.

These systems don't just speak darkness.

They *live* it.

They embed it in language, in facial expressions, in seating arrangements, in who gets to speak and who doesn't.

In those environments, even *truth sounds disrespectful*.

Even *healing feels like rebellion*.

The Symbols We Ignore

Darkness doesn't just speak through words — it speaks through symbols.

- The locked room no one talks about.
- The bruises that "happened from a fall."
- The leader no one questions.
- The child who's always too quiet.

These are not random occurrences.

They are *messages*.

Darkness uses them to test your response.

Will you ask questions?

Will you look closer?
Will you notice what's not being said?

If you do — you become dangerous.
If you don't — you become useful.

Darkness loves useful people.

The Performance of Peace

There is no performance more dangerous than the performance of peace.

It is when the house is decorated but cold.
When the church is full but shallow.
When the family smiles but everyone is bleeding behind closed doors.

In these places, everyone knows what not to say.
Everyone knows what truth to avoid.
Everyone knows how to keep the language of darkness alive — by pretending that light is already present.

But light is not performance.
Light is *presence*.
And it doesn't play by the rules of darkness.

Learning a New Language

To break free from darkness, you must learn to speak a new tongue.

It starts with *truth*.
Not polished, filtered truth. Raw truth.
The kind that makes you tremble a little when you say it.

Then comes *clarity* — naming what was once unnamed.
Followed by *courage* — knowing the cost, and speaking anyway.

Learning this new language won't make you popular.
But it will make you *free*.

And freedom is fluent in light.

Final Reflection

You were never meant to be fluent in fear.
You were never designed to speak in code to survive.
You were not created to dance around truth just to avoid confrontation.

If your language has been shaped by shame, then it's time to unlearn the darkness.

Your voice was not meant for echoing what keeps you bound.
It was meant for calling *things* out — so that others could come *out* too.

Darkness speaks. But so do you.
And when you speak light — darkness loses its audience.

CHAPTER FOUR

Living in the Shadows

You can live in the sunlight and still never see the sky.

You can laugh loudly, work hard, pray often, and still feel like you're buried somewhere beneath yourself—half-alive, half-acting, and fully exhausted.

That's what it means to live in the shadows.

Not in total darkness.
No.
Just close enough to the edge of light that you can pretend you're okay—until someone looks too closely.

The Shadow Life

There is a kind of living that looks like survival but is really just slow surrender.

It's when you smile out of habit, not happiness.
When your "I'm fine" comes faster than your breath.
When your calendar is full but your soul is starving.
When you feel everything and nothing all at once.

This is the shadow life—where you've made peace with dysfunction, where your normal is bruised and bent, but you call it "strong."
Where your identity is wrapped around roles, expectations,

obligations—and your name feels like an alias you can't escape.

People don't always end up in the shadows because of some grand tragedy.
Sometimes, it's just a slow dimming.
A hundred compromises.
A thousand swallowed truths.
A lifetime of pretending.

The Architecture of Internal Darkness

What no one tells you is that sometimes, the darkness isn't *around* you — it's *within* you.

Not because you chose it. But because you were born into it.
Fed it.
Trained to nurture it.
Told it was holy, or humble, or "just how life is."

When you're raised in an environment that shames emotion and silences curiosity, you grow up thinking *feeling deeply is weakness.*

You become fluent in denial.
You apologize when you cry.
You flinch at affection.
You distrust comfort.

Because the shadows taught you:

- Don't speak.
- Don't feel.
- Don't hope.

And worst of all… don't *dream*.

Dreams need light to grow.
And shadows feed on everything that threatens their silence.

Functional Shadows

Many people living in the shadows don't even look broken.

They're teachers. Mothers. CEOs. Pastors. Therapists. Singers. Social workers.

They show up. They perform. They lead.
But deep within, they carry a silence that howls when no one is watching.

That's the thing about functional shadows:
They wear designer clothes.
They smile on stage.
They get awards.
They pray eloquently.

But they go home to numbness.
To overthinking.
To scrolling, drinking, working, performing—anything but sitting still long enough to *feel*.

Because if they stop…
The silence speaks.
The truth surfaces.
And the shadows tremble—because light is trying to get in.

What the Shadows Feed On

Shadows don't just exist. They feed.

They feast on secrecy.

They sip on shame.

They survive off of rituals we don't question:

- The toxic tradition we won't challenge.
- The generational patterns we call "just how we are."
- The relationship that suffocates but we justify it with "loyalty."
- The job that erodes our spirit, but pays just enough to keep us quiet.

Shadows feed on fear—*especially* the fear of being fully seen.

Because to be fully seen is to risk being rejected.

So instead, we stay half-visible.

Half-vocal.

Half-healed.

And we convince ourselves: *"At least I'm still standing."*
Yes… but what if you were born to fly?

The Cost of Staying Hidden

Living in the shadows doesn't just protect you from pain—it protects you from *joy* too.

You can't selectively numb.
When you mute sorrow, you also mute wonder.
When you refuse vulnerability, you shut the door to connection.
When you edit yourself for approval, you lose the parts of you that were meant to shine.

The cost of staying hidden is steep.

You lose time.
You lose clarity.
You lose *you*.

And the longer you stay, the harder it is to imagine life outside of it.

The shadows start to feel like home.
The chains start to feel like comfort.
The ache starts to feel like identity.

But hear me clearly—*you were never meant to stay here*.

How to Come Out

Coming out of the shadows is not an event.
It's a process.
A painfully beautiful one.

It starts with a question:
"Is this really all there is?"

Then comes the whisper:
"There has to be more."

Then the terrifying courage to say:
"I can't stay like this."

You will have to unlearn everything that taught you to survive instead of live.
You will have to grieve the false version of yourself you performed so well.
You will have to disappoint people who loved the shadow version of you.

But oh, the freedom on the other side.

You'll breathe deeper.
You'll speak truer.
You'll sleep cleaner.
You'll laugh harder—not because everything is perfect, but because *you're finally real*.

Final Reflection

If you are reading this and something in you is aching, not for more knowledge but for more *light*—then you are already stepping out.

Don't rush it.
Don't fake it.
But don't go back.

You don't belong in half-truths.
You don't belong in almost-healing.
You don't belong in the shadows.

You were made for full visibility.
For whole-hearted living.
For wide-open wonder.

Some people survive in the shadows.
But you were born to live in the light.
Even if it blinds you at first… keep walking toward it.

CHAPTER FIVE

The Whisper of Light

Light doesn't always arrive with thunder.

Sometimes, it enters like a breath.
Quiet.
Gentle.
Uninvited, but not unwanted.

When you've lived in darkness long enough, light doesn't always feel like a miracle.
Sometimes, it feels like a *threat*—to your comfort, your story, your survival habits.

But it's coming anyway.

Not with a shout.
Not with fanfare.
But with a whisper.

And if your soul is still enough… wounded enough… *ready* enough… you'll hear it.

Not All Light Is Loud

We often imagine light as something overwhelming — blinding, burning, dramatic.
But more often than not, real light arrives quietly.

It shows up in the subtle ways:

- A sentence that shatters your numbness.
- A stranger's honesty that feels like home.
- A dream that keeps returning.
- A moment of stillness where everything you've avoided floats to the surface.
- A child's question you can't answer without weeping.

Light doesn't always roar. Sometimes it *invites*.
It doesn't force the door open.
It waits just long enough for you to reach the handle.

And when you do — even if your hands are trembling — everything begins to shift.

When Light Finds You

Some people chase light.
Others stumble into it.
But the most miraculous moments? That's when light finds *you*.

You weren't looking for healing.
You weren't trying to escape.
You were just trying to *make it to Friday*.

But somehow…
A truth broke through.
A memory returned.
A buried pain surfaced.
And the light whispered:
"You can't stay here anymore."

You thought the darkness had won.
You thought your silence had settled in.
You thought the weight was normal.

But the whisper came — not to shame you, not to expose you, but to awaken you.

The Light Doesn't Lie

Darkness deceives.
Light never does.

That's why it hurts at first.
It shows you *exactly* where the rot is.
Where the bleeding never stopped.
Where the false stories took root.

The light doesn't flatter you.
It *frees* you.

But before it liberates, it reveals.
And that's the part many don't want.

Because it's easier to say, "I'm fine,"
than to admit, "I'm falling apart."
Easier to keep the mask
than to face the mirror.

But if you have the courage to face the truth the light reveals,
you'll find something even more powerful than clarity.

You'll find *mercy*.

Stories of Escape

Every light-bearer was once a captive.
Don't let their strength fool you.

Behind every bold voice is a former silence.
Behind every whole woman is a girl who almost didn't make it.
Behind every fearless man is a boy who cried behind the door no one opened.

And yet…
They heard the whisper.
They followed the flicker.
They trusted the light more than the shame.

They walked out of the system,
left the room,
burned the script,
told the truth.

And their freedom became a roadmap for others.

Because once you've tasted light,
you can never *unknow* its flavor.

The Fear of Stepping Out

The light will call you to step into places you've never walked before.

Forgiveness.
Vulnerability.
Rest.
Boundaries.
Joy.

Yes, joy.
You'd be surprised how terrifying *joy* feels when you've lived in shadow long enough.

Joy feels suspicious.
Peace feels fake.
Stillness feels dangerous.

But those are just echoes of your old world trying to survive in your new one.

The truth is:
You are safe.
You are seen.

And the light has no intention of mocking your wounds — only healing them.

The Choice to Follow

Light is not loud.
It's not forceful.
It will not beg.

It invites.
It waits.
And then it asks a question:
"Will you come with Me?"

You don't have to run.
You don't have to sprint.
You just have to *turn*.

One step is enough.

The light doesn't need spced — it needs surrender.

It needs your *yes* — even if it's whispered through tears, through fear, through trembling lips that have never spoken freely before.

The light knows what it's doing.
It's not afraid of what you carry.
It's not intimidated by your past.
It's not shocked by your secrets.

It came *for you*.

Final Reflection

If you're reading this, and something inside you is stirring — don't ignore it.

That's not just emotion.
That's not a mood.

That is the whisper.

That is light — calling your name.

You may not know how to heal.
You may not know how to break free.
But you *know* you can't keep living the way you've been.

Let that be enough.

Because the whisper of light, once heard, is impossible to unhear.

And once welcomed, it will grow louder.

And brighter.

And kinder.

Until it becomes a voice.

Then a lamp.

Then a sun.

Light doesn't knock the door down.
It whispers.
But if you answer... it will never leave.

CHAPTER SIX

Becoming a Light-Bearer

You were not rescued to remain silent.

Light does not find you, heal you, restore you — just so you can fold your arms and watch others drown.
It does not free you so you can decorate your own peace and ignore those still gasping for theirs.

You were not just *saved from* darkness.
You were *sent back* with something in your hands.

Light.

And that light is not decorative.
It is not ornamental.
It is not fragile.

It is *dangerous*.

To become a light-bearer is to become a disruption.
A walking contradiction to the systems that thrive in

secrecy.

A living, breathing threat to silence.

What Light-Bearers Look Like

They don't always glow.
They don't wear halos.
They don't speak in polished quotes or perfect prose.

Sometimes, they stammer.
Sometimes, they still limp.
Sometimes, their voice shakes when they speak truth — but they speak it anyway.

Light-bearers are often misunderstood, even hated, because their very presence is a confrontation.

They don't just shine light — they *embody* it.
They show what healed looks like.
They expose what hiding looks like.
They remind the room of what it would rather forget.

That's why most people don't clap when the light arrives.
They squint.

They cover their eyes.
They get *angry*.

Because the light disrupts their comfort.
And the light-bearer… reminds them they, too, have a choice.

The Cost of Carrying Light

To carry light is to carry conflict.

You will be loved in secret but rejected in public.
You'll be thanked privately but attacked online.
You'll be accused of exaggerating, of overthinking, of being "too deep," "too honest," "too much."

But still — the light burns.
Still — the truth aches to be told.
Still — your spirit cannot make peace with shadows.

Why?

Because once you've seen too much,
you *can't go back* to pretending.

And the more you shine, the more others begin to see.

That is your reward.

Not applause.
Not perfection.
But clarity — multiplied.
Freedom — shared.
Truth — unleashed.

How to Carry the Light

You don't need a stage.
You don't need a microphone.
You don't need a million followers.

You need integrity.
You need honesty.
You need the courage to live *free* in front of people still bound.

Your healing becomes your testimony.
Your boundaries become your sermon.
Your joy becomes your rebellion.

Let your light come through your art.
Through your parenting.
Through your forgiveness.
Through your refusal to shrink.

Your existence as a whole, free, visible human being… is enough to shake kingdoms.

Because light travels.

And your light is louder than your trauma.

Be Light in the Way You Were Designed

Not every light-bearer preaches.
Some cook.
Some write.
Some build.
Some sit beside the hurting without needing to fix them.

Don't imitate someone else's flame.
Find your own.

Your pain was specific.
So your purpose will be too.

Use what you've seen.

Speak what you've survived.

Shine where others are afraid to look.

The darkness will resist you.

But it cannot contain you.

Because once the light is in you — it's *alive*.

And no one can switch it off but you.

To carry light is to declare war on shadows.
But it is also to offer direction to the lost.
And you, dear reader, are now both a survivor… and a guide.

CHAPTER SEVEN

Light Was Made for War

Let us make one thing clear.

Light is not polite.

It is not passive.
It is not sentimental.
It does not ask darkness for permission before it enters the room.

Light *invades*.

From the moment it appears, darkness is no longer in charge.
It cannot argue.
It cannot delay.
It cannot negotiate.

Because light doesn't ask.
It *acts*.

This is why you've felt the tension.
Why your voice shakes when you speak the truth.

Why old relationships grew cold the moment you set boundaries.

Why the system shifted against you the moment you stepped into clarity.

It's not because you were wrong.
It's because you became a weapon.

Warriors Don't Always Wear Armor

Some of the fiercest warriors carry wounds.

They cry when no one's looking.
They doubt themselves.
They fight in silence.

But they *show up anyway*.

Because they've learned something most people never will:

Light was made to fight.

It was never meant to blend in.
It was never created for decoration.
It was never designed to *coexist* with lies.

Light exists to expose.

To cleanse.

To call out.

To confront.

And to *conquer*.

What Light Destroys

Light tears down altars built to ego.

It breaks cycles masked as tradition.

It strips systems of their fake holiness.

It dismantles reputations built on silence.

It exposes:

- Leaders who manipulate with charm.
- Families who protect abusers.
- Organizations that thrive on oppression.
- Inner worlds where shame has nested like rot in the walls.

Light is not always gentle.

Sometimes it burns.

But only what was never meant to remain.

Why Light Must Be Fierce

We don't just need candles.

We need *torches*.

We need *wildfires* of truth that cannot be contained by culture or hierarchy or false peace.

Because the darkness we face is not passive —

It is strategic.

It is generational.

It is spiritual.

It is organized.

And you don't negotiate with organized darkness.

You confront it.

With flame.

With fire.

With *truth* that makes people uncomfortable.

But also with love that doesn't lie.

With joy that doesn't need permission.

With clarity that cuts without cruelty.

This is war — and light is both weapon *and* victory.

You Are Now the Light

Not just a follower of it.
Not just a fan of it.
Not just a seeker of it.

You *are* it.

The same light that pulled you out… now lives in you.
It guides your words.
It guards your decisions.
It glows in your quiet presence.

And yes — it also makes you dangerous to systems built on shadow.

That's why you will be resisted.
That's why you must never forget what you've survived.

Because your survival was your training.
And your truth is now your sword.

Final Charge

This book is not a conclusion.
It is a commissioning.

It does not end with your healing — it *begins* with your rising.

The world does not need more polished perfection.
It needs more holy disruption.
More people who have seen too much to stay silent.
More people who live like light is not an accessory, but a *mission*.

So shine.
Boldly.
Fiercely.
Softly, if you must — but without apology.

You were never meant to just escape the dark.
You were meant to make darkness regret ever touching you.

Light does not negotiate with darkness.
It invades. It ignites. It liberates.
And now, so will you.

The Blackness of Darkness

By Emma Abbey

"Some truths whisper. Others scream in silence. This book dares to listen."

In a world obsessed with light but terrified of what it reveals, *The Blackness of Darkness* pulls back the veil on the unseen, the unspoken, and the dangerously ignored.

Emma Abbey guides you through the dim alleys of silence, shame, and spiritual sabotage — not as a distant observer, but as one who has walked through the night and lived to name it.

From the subtle seduction of secrecy to the invisible architecture of oppression, this book exposes the systems that thrive in shadow — in families, institutions, faith circles, and within ourselves. Each chapter is a mirror and a map, drawing the reader from exposure to awakening, from surviving to shining.

But this is not just a book about darkness.
It is a call to *war*.
And light — fierce, fearless, unapologetic light — is the weapon.

If you've ever:

- Felt like you're living half-visible in a world that rewards silence,
- Survived what others refuse to speak about,
- Or sensed a call to rise, disrupt, and live in full truth...

Then *The Blackness of Darkness* was written for you.

You weren't meant to just escape the dark.
You were born to confront it.

www.ingramcontent.com/pod-product-compliance
Lightning Source LLC
Chambersburg PA
CBHW050303010526
44108CB00040B/2246